RIGHT NOW

Jessica Olien

BALZER + BRAY
An Imprint of HarperCollins *Publishers*

Balzer + Bray is an imprint of HarperCollins Publishers.

Right Now
Copyright © 2018 by Jessica Olien
All rights reserved. Manufactured in China.
No part of this book may be used or reproduced in any manner whatsoever
without written permission except in the case of brief quotations embodied
in critical articles and reviews. For information address HarperCollins
Children's Books, a division of HarperCollins Publishers,
195 Broadway, New York, NY 10007.
www.harpercollinschildrens.com

Library of Congress Control Number: 2016963491
ISBN 978-0-06-256828-1

Typography by Aurora Parlagreco
17 18 19 20 21 SCP 10 9 8 7 6 5 4 3 2 1
❖
First Edition

For my mom

You are right now.
What are you?

You are a cloud and a ray of light.

You are the tallest tree.

An open door.

A silly dance.

You are as ferocious as a lion

and as sweet as a snail.

Sometimes both at once.

You are a spiderweb.

A sad song.

You are a big puddle, and sometimes people will go around you like they wish you weren't there.

Ignore them.
They don't see your beauty.

But someone does.

You are not bad.
Even when you feel upset.

Or when you make a mistake.

You are the thunder of applause.

A small squeak.

A loud purr.

A belly laugh.

You are a giant yawn.

A happy sigh.

A slice of cake.

A sideways smile.

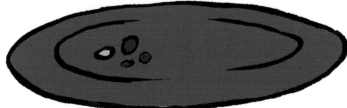

You are big
and small
and loud
and quiet.

The whole universe
lives inside you.

And inside everyone else too.

No matter what you do.

No matter where you live.

Or what you look like.

What will you do with this
collection of things inside you?

Whatever you decide.

But right now you are here.
You are you.

And that is perfect.